Sea   Breezes

Thoughts of God from a Summer Beach

JOHN KILLINGER

ABINGDON PRESS

NASHVILLE

Sea Breezes
Thoughts of God from a Summer Beach

Copyright © 1985 by Abingdon Press

This book is printed on acid-free paper.

Library of Congress Cataloging in Publication Data

KILLINGER, JOHN.
  Sea breezes.
  1. Meditations.
  I. Title.
  BV4832.2.K52   1985   242   84-24538

ISBN 0-687-37088-4

Cover design and illustrations by Nancy E. Johnstone

Manufactured by the Parthenon Press at
Nashville, Tennessee, United States of America

For Annie
whose presence makes any seaside
more beautiful for me

CONTENTS

INTRODUCTION

*T*here is something about the sea—its vastness, its power, its mystery—that always beguiles us. Its attraction for poets and artists is immemorial, and even greater perhaps than for sailors and warriors.

I was a grown man before I saw it. But now, having seen it, I often hunger to see it again. The hunger comes especially when I am tired from too much activity and complexity, from being out of touch with myself. There is a magic in the sea for renewing us at such times, for relieving tension and restoring vision. I can go to the beach for a week and feel revived for half a year.

That is what this book is about—rest and renewal. It is about my own spirit, and how, after a period of overactivity and dryness, I soaked up new life like a sponge. I hope that reading it will help you to feel new life too, even though you may be miles from the ocean.

Nothing in the book was written directly on the beach. I was afraid that would spoil the effects of being at the beach—that I would miss a dozen sensations while trying to capture one in words.

Instead, I followed Herman Melville's advice about

whales, that if one was to hunt them seriously (and today I wish no one did), then one must wound as many as possible when they were discovered and return to kill them at leisure. It was my practice to walk along the beach, or to sit there, and to feel as much and as deeply as I could, and afterwards to sit on the screened porch of our little cabin recollecting in moments of tranquility, as Wordsworth put it, and jotting down my thoughts. This way I not only preserved the sanctity of the beach experience, but had for companionship in my writing the songs of warblers and orioles as they flitted about the scrubby growth outside the porch.

It is inevitable, I suppose that my associations of the beach should be with God. I am a minister, and much of my time is given to thinking of sermons. But my first thoughts, in writing these pages, were always for my personal experience, not for something that might sound good from a pulpit.

If there is a mystery about the sea, I believe it is there not because I am a minister but because it is truly there. And if there is something about that mystery that reminds one of God, it is not because one heard it once in a sermon but because God too is attracted to the sea!

Recovering Sensuality

*I*t is my first day at the beach. I am walking by the water's edge, feeling the wet sand ooze beneath each step. The coconut smell of sun lotion is in my nostrils, and I am vaguely aware of the half-whiteness of my body as I pass bathers whose flesh glistens under a full tan. At the beach, you become conscious of having been out of touch with your body, of having hailed it only occasionally since your last time by the ocean. Life and its manifold duties have conspired to keep you apart, and now here you are, near strangers, with the opportunity of becoming acquainted again.

I remember Sam Keen's having spoken of a "Theology of Carnality." Our religion, he said, has given us too little interpretation of our flesh.

It is true. We have never really understood what it means that our bodies are the temples of the Holy Spirit. With typical piousness, we have assumed only a negative interpretation, that we are to keep our bodies from the obvious sins. We fail to see the more positive side, that we are to keep them fit and trim, and to feel the holy within us, much the way a machine, if it could feel, would feel the very fuel combusting at its center!

It is a middle-class vice that we attach more importance to thinking than to feeling. It bothers us to see the young lolling about in indolence, absorbing the world through their pores. They should be busy, we say, thinking and doing and growing. Yet many of the problems of our culture, from heart disease to our terrible loneliness and isolation, stem precisely from our failure to be at home in our own flesh.

There is something in the *Bhagavad-Gita* about being still and concentrating on the blood flowing in one's toes. That is what I must do at the beach. I must truly feel the sand giving way beneath my feet, and truly smell the scent of coconut oil. I must truly see the sandpipers racing through the surf to capture the retreating mollusks, and truly sense the pressure of heat and sunlight on my temples. It is in all of this that I shall find God again, and know the Holy as more than a statement of dogma.

Sand Castles

*N*early every morning I see the remains of a sand castle some child built high on the beach, hoping the tides would not reach it. They remind me of ruins of ancient castles in England and Scotland, worn down by time and erosion. One sand castle had been especially elaborate, with crenelated towers and improvised flags, a moat and several drawbridges.

Do the children learn from what happens to their castles, I wonder? Does it say something to them about life and time and value? I doubt it. It is we older "children" who see the moral in broken walls and eroded parapets. We see because we have been building castles longer and have seen more of them destroyed.

We have started businesses, erected homes, begun and finished marriages, buried parents and children, and witnessed the tarnishing of dreams. We have entered the day full of hope and retired from it beaten and weary. We have believed in ourselves and our powers of achievement, and have learned that only God is all-powerful and never failing.

Now we are more concerned to lay up treasures in heaven, where rust does not corrupt and sea waters do not break through to destroy.

Rescuing a Horseshoe Crab

*T*his morning I came upon a horseshoe crab washed up by the tide. It was still kicking, feebly, and the wide plate of its underarmor, designed for taking in food, moved in desperate jerks. By now the tide had fallen considerably, and I walked several yards toward the water before flinging back the crab. I watched it lie a moment in shallow water, then kick and float seaward with the next wave.

I felt good about saving the crab. Somehow it seemed a symbol of what life is about—rescuing the creatures who wash up helplessly on life's beaches.

Some are more obvious than others—winos who have no money for food, stranded travelers, divorced persons who speak of suicide because they are so lonely, elderly persons who have no one to look after them and no means to care for themselves.

But there are subtle ones as well—teenagers who are surly and rebellious because they are inwardly alone, good-looking women who have traded for years on their appearance and know it is slipping, outwardly jovial businessmen whose diamond cuff links and Lincoln Continentals cannot entirely mask an inward sense of emptiness and longing, housewives whose apparent composure belies their constant desperation and fear that they are going to break down completely.

They too are horsehoe crabs that need to be thrown back into the water. But not with sermons, only with care and tenderness.

Sea Oats

*T*he sea oats, like nature's flags, wave stiffly from the dunes. "Oh," said a little girl when her mother had named them, "are they for the sea horses to eat?" It was a proper question. I can imagine their coming at night, herds of sea horses galloping upon the beaches, to feed on the strawy grain.

There is too little fantasy in our world today, and too much seriousness. God gave us the gift of imagination as well as the gift of analysis; we should invoke it more often, and smile.

Footprints

I have observed, when following footprints in the sand, that there is a uniqueness about each set. Some people leave deep toe prints, barely touching the rear portion of the foot. Some walk on their heels, so that the toes make only slight impressions. Others walk flat-footedly, distributing their weight evenly over the entire foot. Some prints are blurred, as if their makers rolled their feet in a sideways motion at each step; and some are stamped as neatly as etchings, with every line sharply in focus.

It is impossible not to consider the evanescence of prints. Almost the moment they are formed, the sea begins to lick at them, ready to scatter them to oblivion. The clearer the prints, because closer to the water's edge, the sooner they go.

Thus our mortality follows us, erasing the evidence that we came this way.

I do not find that sad. What a confusing welter of prints there would be, one set on another set, on thousands of other sets, if the prints did not disappear at the rate at which they do!

It is good for the earth to cleanse itself of the life that has existed on it, renewing itself for future generations of men and beasts. Otherwise it would be like a beach house where no families ever leave, though new families continue to move in each week. Soon it would not be fit for anyone's occupancy.

I cannot help remembering, as I follow fresh prints by the water's edge, the story told by Ann Landers about a certain dream a woman had during a stressful period of her life. The woman dreamed that she saw two sets of footprints along the beach, where she and God had been walking together. Then one set ended and only the other remained. The woman was angry with God.

"Where were you when I needed you?" she complained. "You promised never to leave me."

"Oh," said God, "I didn't leave you. That is when I was carrying you."

An Unexpected Benediction

*O*ur sons are sleeping upstairs in the same room. Earlier tonight they were like young puppies, laughing, tussling, and having pillow fights as they did when they were small. One even had a water gun, and that produced squeals and scuffles for a quarter of an hour, until they ruled it out for getting their beds wet. They had not had such fun together for years.

Finally, when tiredness set in and the hubbub began to die, the twenty-year-old called out plaintively, "Does my daddy want to come up and tuck us in?"

What a thrill it gave me! I have not had such an invitation in a long time. Tired as I was, I laid my book aside and mounted the stairs. Blundering through the maze of shoes and twisted clothes on the floor, I made my way in the darkness to each bed and, sitting on its edge, adjusted the sheet and kissed the occupant good night.

They are still talking as I write this. Their spirits are inexhaustible tonight. They do not know what a blessing they have given me.

I think I shall look up in the darkness, when I have gone to bed, and say to my heavenly Father, "Does my Daddy want to tuck me in tonight?"

The Morning After

*M*y bubble has burst! One son admitted to me at the breakfast table that, while I was tucking in the other last night, he was supposed to shoot water on me. Getting me up to their room was all a ruse so they could have fun at my expense.

I laughed when I heard it. It did not really detract from the joy I felt last night. It was only part of their being boys, and full of horseplay. I was honored, in a sense, at being included in the game.

And maybe they didn't really do it after I got there because they loved me and were ashamed to wet me.

I might do the same with God—call Him in on a ruse, then change my mind and let Him quietly tuck me in.

Sunrise

I awoke long before dawn today, and rose to read and write. As the first gray streaks of dawn came into the sky, I took my camera and walked to the beach. As I arrived at the top of the dunes, the red striations of the rising sun were beginning to reach across sky and ocean like a virulent infection. No one else was on the beach. I walked for miles, stopping often to take a picture, or merely to pause and behold the marvelous color gradations on the pitching waves.

Surely there is nothing so awe inspiring as a broad expanse of wet sand, smooth as a mason's trowel, without a solitary footprint to break its spell. I felt as if it were the first day and I alone were present at the creation of the world.

The spell of it all reminded me of Zorba, and how Kazantzakis said each morning he arose and looked at everything—the stones, the trees, the sea, the sky—as if he were looking at it for the very first time, as if God had just created everything during the night. "What is that out there, boss?" he would ask his bookish employer. "That shiny, moving thing? Is that the sea? Is that what it's called, boss?"

Zorba often danced on the beach. He danced when he was happy, and he danced when he was sorrowful. Once, when his three-year-old son died, he danced for hours. If he could not have danced, he said, he would have died.

I thought of my mother in a nursing home, and how she had nearly died three weeks ago. A sunrise is a good place to think about death. Then it is easy to say, "O death, where is thy sting?" The freshness of the air, the color of the sky, the constancy of the waves, all conspire to make me sense the oneness of all things in God.

"We live," said one of my old teachers, "facing a *Western* sunrise!"

The Flounder

*A*s I was walking on the beach at midmorning, I saw a small boy catch a fifteen-inch flounder in the surf. He was so excited that he pulled it through the sand to where his mother was seated with a friend, yelling all the way. She too became excited, and didn't know what to do. I stopped and helped them get the hook out of the fish's mouth. It was a much larger fish, I said to him, than I had seen any grown man catch along the beach.

Walking on down the beach, I reflected on that rare moment. The boy will savor it all his life, regardless of how many great fish he catches in the years ahead. I know, for at the age of six I hooked a large catfish, and I can still recall my breathlessness at realizing I was responsible for such a catch.

Life is a necklace of moments like that.

Seagulls

*G*ulls are masters of the wind. They sculpt it and shape it like matadors gracefully passing the bulls. I have seen them pause in the air for thirty seconds at a time, moving some hidden feather, I am sure, but appearing to remain perfectly motionless, as though frozen in a photograph. Then in an economy of wingstrokes they rise almost instantly to greater heights, whence they come rollercoastering down.

Jonathan Livingston Seagull was a very silly book, on the whole, and the seventeen editors who rejected it before it was finally published were not as derelict as the financial results suggest. But once you got past the silliness it was a very appealing story. The idea of a committed seagull, a sort of Christ figure among gulls, was touching, provided you were in the right frame of mind.

Jonathan learned that being perfect earns one few friends. His incredible dives and rolls and flips made him an outcast among the other gulls. They did not like being shown up by one of their own.

Human nature is like that, even if gull nature isn't. Most

of us do not aspire to fly very high, and we are made uncomfortable by those who do.

How much more sensible it would be to give thanks for the best people we know and learn from them. Then we would all be better off.

Sunburn

I stayed too long in the sun today and now my skin is red and my body is like a stove, giving off heat.

I keep thinking of Daedalus and Icarus, the mythological figures who flew on homemade wings. Icarus flew too close to the sun. The heat melted the wax that held his feathers together, and he plunged into the sea.

I was no nearer the sun today than I ever had been, but the heat got me.

Is it possible to get spiritual sunburn, I wonder, to come too close to God and be damaged by it? Maybe that is how Jesus got himself crucified, and Peter, and Paul. They came so close they were hurt.

I don't think I'll ever get spiritual sunburn, but I would like to. It would be worth the risk of getting hurt. After all, even the sunburn I have gives me a certain pleasure despite the pain.

Overcast Days

*M*any people are disappointed when the clouds come in and there is no sun at the beach. "This is what we're paying $200 a day for?!" they exclaim. "We might as well be at home!"

But overcast days have their value too. They encourage us to stay inside, giving all the cases of sunburn a chance to heal. They provide the openings for many conversations. They inspire bridge games, reading hours, daytime naps, and shopping trips. They cut down on beach clutter. They improve the fishing. And they make clear days all the more precious.

Personally, I enjoy an occasional overcast day, especially if it is produced by a storm and the waves are rolling high. The very bleakness of the world, with the grayness of the sky meeting the grayness of the water, seems to evoke a sense of vitality in the human spirit, as if a spare stage called for bright and lively actors.

Sophoclean drama was like that. The more austere the setting, the more shining and noble the characters who appeared before it.

There are a lot of overcast days in life. Perhaps we should

remember to shine at our brightest when they come, and not be content merely to reflect their grayness.

Like a woman I heard about the other day. She was orphaned at any early age and grew up in a foster home. She was raped by her stepfather. Her husband and three children were killed in a car wreck. She survived the crash as a partial invalid. And at eighty-two, when told that she had inoperable cancer, she said, "Well, you bear what you have to bear."

What a woman for overcast days! And she is right. You bear what you have to bear. But we might as well do it with a song!

Kites

*T*here were a lot of kites at the beach today. Big kites, little kites, yellow kites, green kites, red-white-and-blue kites, dragon kites, bird kites, shield kites, box kites, flat kites, tubular kites, kites with short tails, kites with no tails, kites with tails thirty feet long.

You could tell the inexperienced fliers from the experienced ones. The inexperienced ran with their kites till they were out of breath, they tangled their lines, they crossed the paths of other fliers, they had their kites up and down, mostly down, and they conveyed an impression of being tense, jerky, and ill suited to the business of flying kites.

It occurred to me that they are like people who have trouble with their spiritual lives and who are always making short little runs trying to get their prayer lives up in the air. These people—the ones having trouble with their spiritual lives—are so inexperienced that all their attempts seem awkward and jerky and doomed to failure. They have not learned to relax and let God take their kites up for them, to place themselves in his hands and allow the currents of his generosity to float their spirits upward. Their anxieties dominate their actions, they pull on the line at the wrong time, they overexert themselves in the attempt always to be in control.

When Jesus said, "Be not anxious about tomorrow," he was speaking not only of physical anxieties but of spiritual and emotional anxieties as well, of all those feelings of desperation that we shall not do well in our spiritual natures, that we will choke up and bring our kites crashing to earth again.

The most beautiful people I have ever known, spiritually, have been those for whom the beautiful life seemed almost effortless.

The power to fly or sail gracefully is there in the very air around us. We have but to relax and find the currents that bear us aloft, to let God lift us on swells of spirit. Discipline is important, of course. There is an art to flying kites, and eventually we learn to maneuver them with a slight tug on the line or a flick of the wrist. But learning to trust God to draw us to him is the first thing. After that the discipline comes naturally.

Individualism

I have been reading Oscar Wilde's *De Profundis*, the little book of reflections he wrote in Reading Gaol. I am especially impressed by his description of Christ as "the most supreme of individualists," who, more than any other man who ever lived, possessed his own acts. This was important to Wilde, who was learning in prison to "own" his thoughts and behavior—even to own the crime for which he was incarcerated.

Somehow, I think, that is what I always try to do at the beach—to get in touch with the authentic levels of my being and own my actions. And Wilde leads me to contemplate Christ as the owner of his actions.

Was Christ who he was because he was often at the Sea of Galilee? Because he walked the shore, and sat for hours staring across the shadows and brightness of the waves? Because he traveled in Simon's boat, beholding the shoreline receding and reappearing, and witnessed the frequent miracle of fish being hauled aboard in a net?

Surely it at least contributed to his being the individual he was. And I believe it will contribute to my wholeness as well.

Sunset

I saw a miracle this evening. A glorious sunset overspread the sky, turning the leaden clouds to pink, red, and violet. The churning ocean, lashing deeply at the beach after twenty-four hours of storm, reflected the colors, and the whole world appeared transformed. As the boys and I watched, the colors deepened on the land's horizon, silhouetting the sea oats on the dunes and the occasional gulls overhead. Eventually they became almost blood red—not the color of old blood, but new blood, fresh from the heart and full of oxygen. We had never seen such fiery colors.

I could not help musing on the difference in moods created by such a scene. The day had been cold and gray, and our moods metallic to match. Everyone had been tired, listless, and on edge. One of the boys had remarked at lunch, "Why are we all so grumpy?" It was not even a question; it was a statement of fact.

Now, observing the marvelous sky-fire, we sensed ourselves standing emotionally on tiptoe, filled with awe and excitement. I felt warm and content with my two young men and reached out to entwine arms with both of them. How handsome they were in the glow of twilight, their finely chiseled heads set strongly on tall, slender bodies, their hair curling softly along noble foreheads. I wished their mother were there with us, instead of back in the cabin. She would have liked this miracle, too.

Fat

*Y*ou see a lot of fat at the beach. Oversized people stuffed into diminutive bathing suits. Rolls and lumps and batches of ectoplasm protruding over waistbands, popping out below elastic hemlines, bouncing, jouncing, sagging, flogging, making themselves obvious.

There is nothing like a bathing suit to reveal our sins of the flesh to us and to others. It is even worse in a bathing suit than with total nudity, for those skimpy bits of cloth seem to exaggerate the extent of our corpulence. They are like the little Dutch boy trying to hold back the waters of the mighty ocean with a cramped little finger in the dike. Their very inadequacy only emphasizes the disproportionateness of sagging, uncooperative flesh.

The psalmist was more concerned about fat on the soul—the undisciplined, out-of-control aspect of our inner existence, that places a strain on the spiritual heart just as our overindulged bodies place a strain on our physical hearts. He resolved to get rid of this invisible fat—to diet and exercise it away, to restore himself to spiritual trimness and fitness.

That is something I need to do. I saw myself in a mirror

this morning. I was reading something by Père de Foucauld, the abbot who founded a hermitage in North Africa, and the leanness of his spirit was a challenge to my overweight soul.

I think I will work on myself. I know that spiritual fatness is not as obvious as physical fatness, at least not to others in this age of spiritual obesity. But I know it is there, and I shall not be content until it is gone and I feel myself as taut and trim in my inner life as some of these teenage boys and girls are in their neat little bathing suits. I might even work on my body. Then I would feel good all over and all under too.

The Treasure Hunter

*I*n the twilight tonight I watched the silhouette of a man searching for lost treasures on the beach. He had one of those battery-powered machines with a ring on the end and a beeper to signal the presence of metal objects in the sand. He also had a screen basket on a long handle. Whenever the finder located a hidden object, he scooped through the sand with the basket, usually producing the item he sought in one or two tries.

He reminded me of the parable of the treasure hidden in a field. Jesus said the man in the parable gave up everything he had to buy the field.

Here was a man giving up his evening to search for coins and other baubles in the sand. What would the same man be willing to give to find the kingdom of God?

What would I give?

No More Sea

*I*t is Sunday noon, and I have just returned from a long walk along the ocean. It felt strange, on a comparatively empty beach, not to be in church. I thought of my parish, and of those who would at that hour be gathered to sing hymns and pray and hear the scriptures and sermon.

On the beach, the Holy seemed as real and palpable to me as it ever does in church. And yet I missed something. It was the people, I decided. The Holy might be as real in one place as another, but at the beach the people were missing. On Sunday morning, when they were in church and I here, the separation bothered me.

What did John say in his Revelation about the sea in the afterlife? "And there shall be no more sea." Not because the sea is lacking in beauty or is inexpressive of the majesty and mystery of God, but because the sea is a boundary, a symbol of separation.

No more sea. No more beaches to walk along. No more shells to gather. No more foaming water to swirl at one's feet, retreating with a sucking noise down the plains of sand and pebbles.

But no more separation either. No estrangement because

of envy, resentment, or misunderstanding. No distance between lovers. No miles between brothers and sisters, parents and children, and friends and best friends. No barrier between the living and the dead. All of us together—in God.

For that, I can give up the sea.

Fireworks

I discovered some charred remains of fireworks by the water's edge, and knew the young people had had a party the night before. It was a spectacular display, I am sure, all those explosions of light and color on the perimeter of the ocean's dark expanse.

But how necessary was it really?

I mean, what tiny flickers of light the rockets made when compared with the glow of plankton in the deep or of the full moon rising from the vapors, and how miniscule were the explosions beside the constant thunder of the waves.

God's creation absorbs all our efforts at entertaining ourselves and answers back, "Is that the best you can do?"

Sea Fog

A storm is brewing along the coast, and the air has become unusually warm and humid, producing fog. It obscures boundaries, merging everything into indiscriminate cloud. There is no more sea, no more sky, no more land. Only haze.

Accustomed to definition, I am uncomfortable with this. It is like a drug fantasy in which normal distinctions are blurred, or a nightmare in which everything has an altered value and changed relationships. I feel dizzy and a little frightened.

Religious mystery affects us in much the same way. We much prefer the neat orthodoxies with which we usually live to the sudden confusion of emotions when God absorbs us into the divine presence. The anonymous author of *The Cloud of Unknowing* understood this. "The presence threatens us to the very core of our beings," he said, "because it unsettles all our judgments about the way things are."

Perhaps this is why there is no one alive more daring than the mystic—not a mountain climber, not an astronaut, not a race-car driver, not a soldier of fortune. The mystic alone enters where he has absolutely no control, but must surrender totally to otherness. He or she alone braves possible death of soul—a far greater peril than mere death of body.

And, proportionately, the rewards of the mystic are far greater than those of any other adventurer. If he succeeds, his darkness becomes light indeed, and his confusion indescribable ecstasy!

Scavenging

*T*here are few pleasures I know more harmless or filled with more childlike delight than combing the beach for shells or other produce of the sea. I am a born scavenger, a dreamer that I shall come upon something for nothing.

When I was a child, I knew I should be the one to find the gold at the end of the rainbow. As an adolescent, I fully expected to discover a way of trisecting an angle with a straight edge and a compass, a deed my tease of a geometry professor assured us would fetch a million dollars. Even now, I always go to the mailbox with a lilting confidence that it contains illustrious news of some kind.

It is important, I think, that I am never dejected or downcast that nothing comes of my dreams and expectations. It is not attaining or winning that counts; it is the dream itself, the lure, the sense of heightened expectancy!

It takes little to satisfy me completely. If I found a quarter, when I was a child, it was as overwhelming to me as if it had been the gold at the end of the rainbow. The "A" I received in geometry class quite sufficed for the million dollars. And now, taking the bills and circulars from the mailbox, I find some kind of mystic poetry in being addressed as "Occupant"!

Shuffling along the beach, I need no tide-borne treasure maps to send me into delirium. A few nicely polished shell fragments or a piece of colored glass from some old ship's window will do quite handsomely, thank you.

Silhouettes

*A*fter the sun had doffed its robe of many colors this evening, and had settled to rest behind the horizon, I sat for a while watching the darkened silhouettes of trees and people against the backdrop of fading light. They were like cardboard cutouts, two-dimensional objects in a viewing gallery.

What is it that gives people their third dimension, their fully human existence? It is the light. Without it we are flat, sterile, lacking. But with it the possibilities are endless. Not only do we live in three dimensions, we smile and cry and wave and dance and hug and leap and bow and exist in all our individual personhoods.

This is what makes Jesus' statement "I am the light of the world" so important. His great humanity throws such light on ours that we are cast into ultra-dimensional existence.

Full Moon

*T*here is a full moon over the ocean tonight, and the waves thrash and heave in a nocturnal loving. What is there about the moon that is so magical and romantic? Surely it is the influence of a heavenly body so near to us. Small as it is, the moon exerts considerable force upon the earth and its residents. Old-timers are probably right about its effect on crops, and the police say they are busier on nights when the moon is full.

I'm sorry in a way that men ever arrived at the moon. I hate to think of the debris that has been left on its surface. It is like beer cans around Walden Pond or fast-food cartons under the buttresses of Notre Dame. Nothing is sacred any more, or safe from the desecrating presence of tourists.

But the Bible says that the moon will praise God, and I suppose it will, even littered with junk from our space trips. Outside of heaven itself, all praise is probably alloyed with non-praise. God could have made it different if he had wanted to.

Seashells

*M*illions of miracles wash up on beaches every day. They are called seashells. Actually they are hardened deposits of calcium carbonate secreted by marine creatures known as mollusks and later abandoned by the mollusks. The miracle is that they are formed in such splendid variety and with such incredible symmetry and beauty.

My first acquaintance with the sea was through a huge conch shell that belonged to a friend in my childhood. I loved to put my ear to the open side of the shell and listen to what I then believed to be the roar of the waves. Somehow, I thought, the magic of the infinite deep had been captured in that finite shell, imprisoned in it the way one places fireflies in a jar.

I am still a sucker for shells. I can stroll the beach for hours, turning up this specimen and that, stooping to wash the sand from the nacreous belly of one or pausing to catch a glint of sunlight on another.

There is a sense in which "the magic of the infinite deep" is caught in all of them, for they bespeak a creative power of unspeakable glory and imagination. The beauty of a single shell is enough to convince me of the presence of a divine hand shaping the world. In their proliferative abundance, they ought easily to persuade the most hardened or confused agnostic. A pocketful of shells is a pocketful of arguments for the existence of God.

More than that, for me.

Carried home and spread out on the table, they are reminders of the presence of God right there in the room where I am. I tremble when I touch them, for I know that I am not alone.

Shipwreck

I have been reading an account of the many shipwrecks on the Outer Banks. There is something terribly fascinating about stories of naval disaster. Perhaps they call up memories of tales by Daniel Defoe and Robert Louis Stevenson.

When we were living in England, I heard Colin Morris interview Derek Scott, a heroic and often decorated lifeboatman with the Royal Coastguard, in an intriguing conversation. The lifeboatman's job, whenever there is a storm and some boat is endangered or wrecked on the coast, is to pull on his Wellingtons and slicker and go out to the rescue.

Morris drew a deep breath at the thought of going out on a dark night in a mere lifeboat, with the wind driving the rain and heaving the waves into twenty-five-foot swells.

"Did you ever not go?" he asked.

"Almost, once," came the reply.

It was shortly after Scott had married. There was a terrible storm, and the waves were unusually high. The winds were howling and slates were flying off the roof. Word came of a vessel in distress. His wife said no, he couldn't possibly go; she had had a premonition of his not returning.

He couldn't not go, he said.

He went into the bedroom to get a sweater. As he pulled the sweater over his head, he heard the key clicking in the lock. His wife had locked him in.

An argument ensued, through the door. She would not relent. She had had presentiments, she insisted.

"But if I do not go," he said, "they will be lost. You don't want someone's death on your conscience, do you?"

Finally she opened the door.

"And did you save someone?" asked Morris.

"Oh yes," said Scott, "several."

How many families of men lost in shipwrecks would have been glad for such a heroic rescuer in their vicinity!

I tremble when I think of what going to sea once meant. In Amsterdam, I have seen the House of Tears, where wives and children once stood to bid their loved ones good-bye as their ships glided out of the harbor. None of them more than half hoped to see their menfolk again.

Irish sweaters are still knitted in the coarse yarns and unique designs of old family patterns, slow to disintegrate in salt water, that served to identify many a sailor whose decomposed body washed ashore from the sea.

We live in a safer time, in most respects. The coast is dotted with teenagers on surfboards and inner tubes, with pleasure-seekers in sailboats and private fishing vessels. Ocean voyagers travel on luxury liners equipped with radar and high-powered radios. The sea is much less threatening, except in times of hurricane.

The effects on our spiritual temper are considerable. The illusion gains ground that we are our own masters and have no need of God. We are like the blackbird of the Italian proverb who cries at the close of January, "I fear thee no more, O Lord, now that the winter is behind me."

Perhaps wrecks serve the purpose of reminding us of the terror men once felt when setting out to sea—the kind so palpable in the little whaling chapel described in *Moby Dick*, where Father Mapple climbed into the pulpit shaped like a ship's prow and pulled up the ladder after him.

"What could be more full of meaning?" asked Melville,

> for the pulpit is ever this earth's foremost part; all the rest comes in its rear; the pulpit leads the world. From thence it is the storm of God's quick wrath is first descried, and the bow must bear the earliest brunt. From thence it is the God of breezes fair or foul is first invoked for favorable winds. Yes, the world's a ship on its passage out, and not a voyage complete; and the pulpit is its prow.

It is hard to stand on a reef by one of these old wrecks, worn and enfeebled by the years of tides, and not feel a sense of reverence. If not for God and the sea, at least for the men who once put out in ships the size of these.

Sand Daisies

I had never seen sand daisies before coming to this beach. They are nearly crimson, and much more like the sun, or day's eye, for which the flower was named, than ordinary daisies. The sandy soil, I suppose, makes them that way. Thus everything in the world is unique according to the soil of its environment, and therefore to be treasured. I dislike homogenization, whether in art, society, or religion. Variety is the chief glory of creation.

Bathing Suits

I've been observing the bathing suits people wear at the beach. There are hundreds of varieties. It must tax the ingenuity of designers to produce constantly new combinations of patterns and shapes—especially as the focus of design becomes increasingly diminutive.

The stress factor on some of those little suits is another thing. Why, the Golden Gate bridge isn't under such tension! You only wonder how their occupants get into them. Maybe they stretch them on special machines and then squeeze themselves in with the aid of oversized shoehorns.

We have come almost full circle now. Adam and Eve were nude in the garden. Today, after the prudery of Puritanism and Victorianism, we have returned to an approximation of nudity.

What does Genesis say? After Adam and Eve ate the fruit, they "knew they were naked, and were ashamed." But not the wearers of modern bathing apparel. In fact, most of them seem quite proud of the abundance of flesh they display. They laugh and toss their heads and flaunt their bodies—their white, pink, red, brown, sallow, tan, underweight, overweight, tight, flabby, old, young, middle-aged bodies—as if they were $18-a-pound smoked salmon at a buffet party.

That is good, I think. People should be at peace in their bodies, and that means not feeling any shame about their appearance in a bathing suit. I only wish some of them had a little more sense of aesthetic, and chose suits more appropriate to their shapes and sizes. Even they might appreciate the improvement when they regard themselves in the mirror.

Sea Breezes

*S*urely nothing is more delightful, on a hot summer's day, than a cool breeze blowing in from the sea. It not only refreshes the skin of one's body, it carries the scent of salt air as well, producing relaxation in both mind and flesh.

Once I overheard an old gentleman on a ship remark that he liked "wind off of deep water." I had the impression that he was speaking of something spiritual as well as physical, that he was thinking of the mysteries of life and their nourishing function in our daily existence.

Maybe that is why we like the sea. Its unexplored depths cradle incalculable secrets, and, in a world as thoroughly mapped and documented as ours is coming to be, we are drawn to the edge of the unknown, where we remember our finitude and feel like worshiping again. Here the sea breezes whisper of eternity, and of all those aspects of the self and its place in the universe that we tend to forget in our workaday worlds. They remind us of God and restore hope to our troubled hearts.

Here at the beach people walk and think about their lives. They remember their childhoods and dream about their futures. They recall loved ones who have died and enjoy the children who seem far from death. They repent of mistakes and resolve to live differently when they go home. They think about things that matter. They get in touch with life's intangibles.

Thank God for beaches, and thoughts about life, and the chance to begin again. Thank God for sea breezes!

Bobwhite

I was awakened this morning by a bobwhite outside our window. It had been years since I heard one so clearly. I lay there thinking of the times I had heard one when I was a boy, and imagining for a few moments that I was a boy again. Are we that close to innocence, that a bird can call us back again?

Laziness

I have felt lazy all day today. Torpor rules in my body like a drug. Everything around me seems to move in adagio, as if it were a ballet occurring in slow motion. It feels good, actually, like some gradual therapy to offset the pace and stress of my normal existence.

I think God intends for us to be lazy part of the time. The Puritans, who championed a work ethic, were bad theologians, overemphasizing the depravity of man and the importance of working to stay out of trouble. They did not realize that much of the trouble in the world is trouble we work ourselves into, not trouble that occurs because we have nothing to do.

Lying in the sun or strolling absent-mindedly down a lane of beach houses does not incline my mind to evil thoughts. On the contrary, I feel the presence of God around me as if it were a warm liquid bearing me up in a dream. Healing is taking place inside me, and the laziness is part of my recuperation.

I like to pretend that I will never return to work. I know that I shall, of course, and indeed will be gnawing at the bit in a few days to do so. But for now it is a marvelous fantasy, as though I were Adam relaxing in Eden after naming all the animals, sipping a cool drink and thinking, "God, this is nice, it must be Paradise. If I'm dreaming, God, don't wake me up."

Cypress Trees

*T*he cypress trees on the beach stand in clumps growing from the same root, like family groupings that came for a picnic years ago and never went home. How smooth and cool their gnarled trunks are! What wonderful shelter they offer at midday from the hot sunlight!

They have seen many storms, I fancy, and have heard years of ferocious waves crashing against the shore.

That is the way families ought to be, standing close together when the storms and waves come. They shelter one another from the worst that nature can do, and support one another when the hard winds blow.

The Breakers at Night

*E*ven in deepest darkness they are there, the breakers, pounding, pounding, pounding. "Evidence of things unseen." The surging, unwitnessed, does not hesitate.

So God continues his gifts to us even when we cannot see or feel that they are there. Even in the dark night of the soul, when faith seems as foreign as feeling to a stone.

When daylight returns, we see them. And we know they have been there all along.

Beach Party

*T*hey laugh and sing and hold hands around a blazing fire. Their conviviality warms the night air and sends waves of joy up and down the beach.

They have come for the ocean, presumably, but seem not to notice it as the talk grows more boisterous and the meat sizzles over the flames.

Can they have forgotten the infinite dynamo surging there in the shadows, its cold, wet arms clawing endlessly to hold on to the sand? Or is the human consciousness simply incapable of remaining aware?

I wonder.

I remember a night years ago when I walked along a beach in southern New Hampshire. It was the final night of the season, and revelers were enjoying a last fling before the closing of the shops and restaurants and shooting galleries along the boardwalk. Hardly anyone was on the beach. Only a few lovers who preferred the darkness or the rhythmic cascade of the waves to the electronic chaos of the boardwalk.

I was indignant at the masses. What right had they to elect the boardwalk over the dark majesties of nature? It was, I decided, a parable. Most people prefer the hurdy-gurdy of the present, the brightly lit fun spots of the temporal, to the somber beauties of eternity.

That is true, I suppose. But now I am less sure it is a bad thing. Maybe it is part of the business of being human. I certainly despise humanity less than I did then, have a greater tolerance for it. "The human comedy," Balzac called it. And it is. A comedy in the sense of a spectacle, an act, a theatrical production. We are something to behold, building our bonfires on the edge of such an infinite night and ignoring it as if it weren't there.

It may be the best way of preparing for the night. I cannot say, for I have never been much of one for parties. But the older I get the more I appreciate them. They have their place in the scheme of things.

Driftwood

I have always loved driftwood. Even before I ever saw a beach, I admired it in the homes of those who had carried it back from vacations in Florida or Louisiana. To touch it made me feel that I was momentarily connected with some great mystery, with faraway places and unknown depths of the sea.

What character it has! Rolled and etched and made smooth by years in the water, it is reduced to its essential nature. There is nothing extraneous on it, no soft or pulpy exterior, no deceptive façade. It is what it is, the bare core of itself.

It is what I wish I were, in a spiritual way. I hope the years in God's presence will do that to me, will strip away the false or unnecessary parts of my existence, and cut and polish my being until it is hard and lean and full of character. Prayer, as I understand it, works that way on the human spirit. We are washed this way and that by the tides of the Holy, giving up parts of the self that are soft and expendable, until at last we are strong, trim, and pared to the essence of ourselves. Then we are really suited for eternity. Then it gives God pleasure to touch us.

On Going Home

*W*hy is it that vacations always seem to end just as you have really begun to enjoy them? "I wish we were only starting our vacation now," said my wife as we were packing to go home. "I finally feel rested enough to appreciate it."

The trouble is, of course, that we work so hard all year that it takes us a couple of weeks or so to wind down once we get away from the house and the job and all the responsibilities at home. Then it is time to start back.

This should be a warning to us to slow down at home and enjoy some of the qualities of a good vacation—the feeling of relaxation, the mood of discovery, the time to read and reflect and get reacquainted with ourselves and our families—all year long.

With increasing frequency, Americans seem to be losing this capacity. Maybe it is TV that is to blame—the incessant presence of noise, violence, and chatter in our lives. Or maybe life is simply getting harder all the time—more traffic on the highways, more demand in our jobs, more personal property to care for, more pressure socially, even higher expectations within our family relationships. Whatever the cause, most of us are not very successful at maintaining a sense of grace and relaxation in our daily living, and we depend on vacations for the decompression that will salvage our existence.

This is where our religious practice ought to produce some healthy changes in us. The few minutes we spend in prayer and quiet meditation each day can become the restorative center of our total beings. From this gentle oasis in the midst of our hurry and worry there can evolve the spirit of relaxation and self-possession that will revolutionize who we are and how we regard life itself. This time of daily devotion, consistently followed, can do the work of a perpetual vacation by lubricating our minds and hearts with a sense of the eternal in the midst of all the clamor and confusion of secular existence.

Then, when we really do go on vacation, we will be ready to enjoy it from the very first. And, when the vacation is over, we will not hate to go home, for home will mean a continuation of what is best about the vacation.